THE AMERICAN FLAG

AMERICAN SYMBOLS

Lynda Sorensen

The Rourke Book Company, Inc.
Vero Beach, Florida 32964

PHOTO CREDITS
© Lynn M. Stone: cover, title page, pages 8, 13; courtesy National Park Service: page 4; © Reinhard Brucker: page 7; © Frank Balthis: page 15; courtesy U.S. Marine Corps: page 18; courtesy U.S. Army Military History Institute: pages 10, 12; courtesy NASA: page 17; courtesy Flagsource, J.C. Schultz Enterprises, Inc.: page 21

ACKNOWLEDGEMENTS
The author thanks J.C. Schultz Enterprises, Inc., St. Charles, Illinois, for its cooperation in the preparation of this book.

Library of Congress Cataloging-in-Publication Data

Sorensen, Lynda, 1953–
　　The American flag / by Lynda Sorensen
　　　　p.　cm. — (American symbols)
　　Includes index.
　　ISBN 1-55916-048-9
　　1. Flags—United States—Juvenile literature. [1. Flags—United States] I. Title II. Series.
CR113.S57 1994
929.9'2'0973—dc20　　　　　　　　　　94–7050
　　　　　　　　　　　　　　　　　　　　　　CIP
Printed in the USA　　　　　　　　　　　AC

TABLE OF CONTENTS

THE AMERICAN FLAG

"Old Glory," as the American flag is sometimes called, stands for the United States of America. Like any flag, it is just a piece of cloth. But this is cloth with powerful meaning.

Flapping in the wind, this red, white and blue cloth has made people feel joy and hope. It has stirred men to battle and helped them enjoy victory. It has brought tears of happiness and pride to countless eyes.

The U.S. flag at the Washington Monument: powerful message in red, white and blue

THE FIRST AMERICAN FLAG

Americans fought the Revolutionary War (1775-1783) to gain their freedom from England. Leaders of the **revolution** wanted a flag to represent the new country.

The first American flag was chosen on June 14, 1777. It had 13 red and white stripes and 13 stars on a blue background. The 13 stars and the 13 stripes stood for the 13 English colonies in America. At that time they were fighting to become the United States of America.

A 27-star flag flies over Bent's Old Fort, remade to look as it did in the 1840's

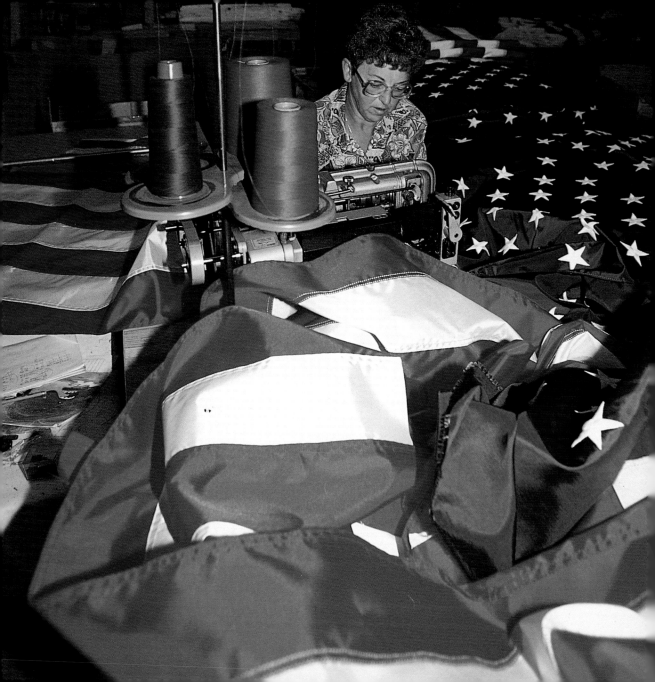

THE DESIGNER OF THE FIRST FLAG

No one knows who really designed the first American flag. A legend that Betsy Ross made the first flag is probably false. Betsy Ross, a Philadelphia **seamstress**, did sew flags during the Revolutionary War. No proof exists that she designed or sewed the first flag.

It is likely that Francis Hopkinson had a part in designing the first flag. Mr. Hopkinson was one of the signers of the Declaration of Independence.

A modern seamstress making U.S. flags

CHANGES IN THE FLAG

By 1794 two more states had joined the original 13. Two stars and two more stripes were added to the flag. By 1818 five more states had been added. **Congress** decided that 20 stripes would be too many on the flag. Congress voted to return to the original 13 red and white stripes. Each new state was shown by the addition of a star.

The present flag has 50 white stars, one for each of the 50 states.

This torn U.S. flag, held by a Union soldier, survived battle during the Civil War

An American flag covers the coffin of President John F. Kennedy who was murdered in 1963

Awash in a sea of stars and stripes, a seamstress puts finishing touches on Old Glory

THE FLAG UNDER FIRE

After the Revolutionary War, the United States fought the War of 1812 with England. During the war, Francis Scott Key wrote the words to the *Star Spangled Banner.*

One day in September, 1814, Key, a lawyer, sailed toward a British warship outside Baltimore Harbor. Key was trying to win the release of a British prisoner.

That night Key watched a fiery sky as British ships fired cannons at Fort McHenry in Baltimore Harbor.

A 15-star flag, like the one Francis Scott Key saw, still waves over rebuilt Fort McHenry

THE "STAR SPANGLED BANNER"

The British cannons quit firing some time during the night. Key wondered if Fort McHenry had surrendered.

"By the dawn's early light," Key had his answer. The "stars and stripes" still waved over Fort McHenry.

Key was overjoyed. He wrote a poem to celebrate. He titled it the *Star Spangled Banner*—a flag glittering with stars.

In 1931 the *Star Spangled Banner* became America's national **anthem**, or song.

One hundred and fifty-eight years after Francis Scott Key watched the stars and stripes over Fort McHenry, John Young planted the flag on the moon

THE FLAG AT WAR

During the American Civil War (1861-1865) soldiers from the Northern states carried the American flag into fierce battles. Southern soldiers carried the flag of the Confederate States of America. The flags stirred both sides to battle.

Eighty years later the American flag was still flying on a battlefield. American Marines proudly raised Old Glory after the vicious battle with Japanese soldiers on Iwo Jima in 1945.

The Iwo Jima Monument recalls the U.S. Marines' flag-raising after their bloody victory on that island in 1945

RESPECTING THE FLAG

The United States flag code is a set of rules for honoring the flag.

The code says the flag can be flown in daylight whenever bad weather is not likely to damage it. The flag is usually flown from sunrise to sunset. A flag flown at night should be spotlighted.

The flag should never be worn as clothing, and it should never touch the ground.

A huge American flag, 100 feet long and 50 feet wide, stretched nearly nine stories on the Wrigley Building in Chicago, 1991

FLAG DAYS

Flag Day is celebrated each June 14, the birthday of the American flag. On Flag Day Americans display flags at homes, schools, businesses and public buildings. Groups that promote love and respect for the flag hold parades to honor the flag.

Certain holidays are also "flag days." Americans display large numbers of flags on the Fourth of July, Memorial Day and Veterans Day.

Each flying American flag is a reminder of a proud, strong and free nation.

Glossary

anthem (AN thum) — a sacred hymn or song

congress (KAHN gress) — a body of lawmakers representing, in the United States, the states

revolution (REH vo lu shun) — an uprising by people against their own government; a revolt

seamstress (SEEM stress) — a woman whose job is sewing

INDEX